My Party

Devised by Maoliosa Kelly
Photographed by Steve Lumb

Collins

2

5

6

My Party

Ideas for reading

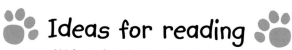

Written by Clare Dowdall, PhD
Lecturer and Primary Literacy Consultant

Learning objectives: talk about the book, identifying major points and key themes; use a variety of cues when reading; use language to imagine and recreate roles and experiences; use talk to organise, sequence and clarify thinking, ideas, feelings and events.

Curriculum links: Personal, social and emotional development: be confident to try new activities and speak to a familiar group

Getting started

- Look at the front cover of the book and read the title together. Ask the children about their experiences of parties.

- Ask the children to imagine what might happen in this non-fiction book. Support this by asking about the different stages of the party: e.g. the preparation; the guests' arrival; the games.

- Walk through the pictures with the children and discuss what is happening on each page.

Reading and responding

- Ask the children to read the book together from the beginning. As there are no words to read, ask them to describe the stages of the party using the pictures.

- Encourage the children to look at each picture carefully. Provide new vocabulary where necessary to help children discuss their ideas.

- Encourage the children to compare the pictures to their own experience of parties. Dwell on pp4–5 and share ideas about favourite party food. (Sensitivity to the range of children's cultures and experiences may be needed here.)